"TAKE ME OUT TO THE BALL GAME"

and Other Favorite Song Hits 1906–1908

Edited by
LESTER S. LEVY

DOVER PUBLICATIONS, INC.
New York

Copyright © 1984 by Dover Publications, Inc.
All rights reserved under Pan American and International Copyright Conventions.

Published in Canada by General Publishing Company, Ltd., 30 Lesmill Road, Don Mills,
Toronto, Ontario.
Published in the United Kingdom by Constable and Company, Ltd.

"Take Me Out to the Ball Game" and Other Favorite Song Hits, 1906–1908 is a new work, first
published by Dover Publications, Inc., in 1984. It consists of unabridged, unaltered republica-
tions of the sheet music of 23 popular songs (original publishers and dates of publication are
indicated in the Contents) and an Introduction by Lester S. Levy.
The publisher is grateful to Mr. Levy, to the Enoch Pratt Library, Baltimore, and to the
Eisenhower Library, Johns Hopkins University, for lending the original sheet music for reproduc-
tion.

Manufactured in the United States of America
Dover Publications, Inc., 31 East 2nd Street, Mineola, N.Y. 11501

Library of Congress Cataloging in Publication Data

Main entry under title:

Take me out to the ball game.

   Songs reprinted from original sheet music eds.
   1. Songs with piano.   2. Music, Popular (Songs, etc.)—United States.
I. Levy, Lester S.
M1619.T17   1984   83-20544
ISBN 0-486-24662-0

PREFACE

The years are 1906–1908. The United States was quiet, the people for the most part contented. The work force was nearly fully occupied. Similar conditions obtained among our friends across the Atlantic, Great Britain, Germany, Russia, France and Italy.

Musically we were attracted to good show songs, but even more hits were introduced by popular singers on the vaudeville stage. We also enjoyed tuneful popular music from abroad, just as the Europeans welcomed, and occasionally employed, our own composers.

The piano business here was an important industry. Its manufacturers sold their products by the thousands. There was a piano in every respectable home, and in many that were not so respectable. Department stores and "five and dimes" had special music departments, with hundreds of songs displayed for the interested customer. Seated at a piano in each department was a female performer. If a shopper were to pick up a piece of music with an attractive cover and say, "May I hear how this goes?," the performer would run through the song, and if the shopper liked it she would pay her ten cents or a quarter; another purchase was completed. If the piece had no appeal to her there was no obligation to buy, nor any charge for the rendition.

George M. Cohan was in his heyday; Victor Herbert was a name to be conjured with. But Irving Berlin had not commenced to write until 1906, and in that year he contributed the lyrics for just one song which was quickly forgotten. His published musical composition was nonexistent until three or four years later. And Jerome Kern was just starting to add a song or two to someone else's musical. George Gershwin was a small boy, not yet in his teens. The great hits "Old Man River" and "There's No Business Like Show Business" were twenty and forty years away.

But the music fans of 1906, 1907 and 1908 had their own favorites: Gus Edwards, Will D. Cobb, Jack Norworth, Nora Bayes, Albert Von Tilzer, Kerry Mills.

This book contains hits produced by these and other successful writers during the three years that were among the finest of the flowering of popular music. The pieces introduced include a few brought over from London, Paris, Berlin and Vienna.

As a starter we'll present the all-American hero, George M. Cohan. Way back in 1868 a promising young comedian named Jerry Cohan was appearing in minstrel shows. Eventually he married, and in due time became the father of two children, one of whom, George, was born in Providence in 1878. The life of the entire family centered on the theater and the vaudeville stage. They appeared together and were billed as "The Four Cohans."

George wrote his first song at the age of sixteen, and by his twenties he was one of the great stars of the American stage, and could write the catchiest words and music for the shows in which he was the principal performer and most proficient dancer.

From 1900 on George was writing musical shows, including all the lyrics and music, and was a singing, dancing comedian with an enormous following. Cohan fans may especially remember his 1917 World War I hit, "Over There," but in the dozen years between his start and this great battle cry, he continued to entrance his audiences. Songs like "Harrigan" in this volume had wondrous appeal.

Another great name of the period, in fact over a period of several decades, was Victor Herbert. Herbert, in addition to being a prolific and engaging composer, had a varied musical career. Born in Ireland in 1859, the grandson of a distinguished Irish novelist, composer and artist, he followed his grandfather's advice and went to Germany for his general and musical education. In due time he became first cellist of the Stuttgart Court Opera, where he also acquired the technique of composition. In 1886 Walter Damrosch brought him to America where he became a cellist in, and later assistant conductor of, the Metropolitan Opera Company.

Herbert's first operetta appeared in 1894 and he continued to write for thirty years thereafter. In 1908 his loveliest numbers included "Love Is Like a Cigarette" and "Ask Her While the Band Is Playing," both of which are reproduced in this book.

Some of the greatest music of the era was written by the brothers Harry and Albert Von Tilzer. Each was prominent on his own as a prolific composer and as a song publisher. Both men got into music by the "back door." Harry's early days were spent in a circus; Albert was a shoe buyer in a Brooklyn department store. But these were only preliminary jobs before they settled on their lifetime goals. Music was to the Von Tilzers the cream in their coffee.

One of Albert's early confederates was young Jack Norworth. In 1908 they joined forces in what turns out to be as immortal a popular song as any written during the last seventy-five years, "Take Me Out to the Ball Game." As long as professional baseball reigns as the leader of all American sports, there will never be a pre-game warm-up by the hometown pitcher which is not preceded by this song; it is as symbolic of baseball as the Stars and Stripes are of a parade. It is difficult to believe—but true—that Von Tilzer never witnessed a baseball game until twenty years after the song was written.

The pair that everyone admired, Norworth and Nora Bayes, each a star on the vaudeville stage, were married in 1907. The semiroyal wedding, vicariously delighting millions of Americans, was seized on quickly by the impresario Florenz Ziegfeld. The newlywed team had written a catchy ballad called "Shine On, Harvest Moon," one often revived and still sung by barbershop quartets. Ziegfeld, who a year earlier had started to produce his annual *Follies*, knew he would add an enormously successful act to the 1908 production if he could engage Bayes and Norworth to appear and give the public "Shine On, Harvest Moon." So the deal was struck, and the darlings of the stage helped Ziegfeld pull off one of his most delightful numbers.

Will D. Cobb and Gus Edwards were another team that ran smoothly through one hit after another. In 1907 their inspirational boy-and-girl waltz "School Days" was unquestionably the hit of the year and the most successful of the many numbers that this pair produced. Edwards, incidentally, soon thereafter switched his principal vocation to stage productions and performances. He gathered together for his acts a group of youngsters whom he called "school boys and girls," and their performances marked the high spot of every vaudeville show in which they appeared. Among those who got their start on the road to fame as members of Gus Edwards' various children's troupes were Eddie Cantor, George Jessel and Walter Winchell.

Kerry Mills, who composed the music for "Red Wing," had scored ten years earlier with the most popular cakewalk of the day, "At a Georgia Campmeeting," and in 1904 had added to his already established fame with "Meet Me in St. Louis." Indian subjects had begun to beguile the public and Mill's "Red Wing" was one of the period's hits in this field.

We cannot overlook the composers born abroad. One was Karl Hoschna, who came here as a brilliant oboist from Bohemia before he was twenty, and was soon playing in orchestras led by Victor Herbert. Before 1908 his compositions were recognized as Broadway material. In that year he teamed with Otto Hauerbach to give us one of the musical hits of the year, *Three Twins*. Two of the most successful songs from that show were "Cuddle Up a Little Closer, Lovey Mine" and "The Yama-Yama Man," and both are included in this volume.

An even more successful European composer was Franz Lehár. Born in Hungary in 1870, trained as a violinist, accomplished as a bandmaster, he turned to composition, and was launched in Vienna with the brilliant *Die lustige Witwe*. With English words and the title *The Merry Widow* it came to New York, where theatergoers were enraptured by the rich melodies. Three of them will be found here as you turn the pages.

The writers of other hits of the years 1906, 1907 and 1908 should at least receive mention in this short preface, but for the sake of brevity the background of only some of the most important songwriters has been summarized.

Look backward now to the music of seventy-five years ago.

LESTER S. LEVY

NOTE

No cover is reproduced for three of the songs in this volume because they have series covers prepared for entire shows, and these shows are represented elsewhere in the book. Thus, "Love Is Like a Cigarette" is from *Algeria*, and the cover for that show appears on page 1, where it serves as the cover for another song from *Algeria*, "Ask Her While the Band Is Playing." "Vilia" has the same *Merry Widow* cover as "I Love You So" (page 30). "The Yama-Yama Man" has the same *Three Twins* cover as "Cuddle Up a Little Closer, Lovey Mine" (page 10).

In addition, "To Maxim's Then I Go" has no cover because it is reproduced from a booklet rather than from a song sheet.

CONTENTS

The songs are arranged in strict alphabetical order by using their titles as printed on the first page of music of the original sheets (not counting "A" or "The" at the beginning of the title). The publishers given here (abbreviated "Pub.") are those indicated on the covers of the specific first or early editions being reprinted. The years given are those of copyright.

Mr Frank McKee Presents The Musical Play

Algeria

Book and Lyrics by
Glen MacDonough

Music by
Victor Herbert

Chas. K. Harris
New York   Chicago   London.

Ask Her While The Band Is Playing.

Millicent and Female Chorus.

Lyric by
GLEN MAC DONOUGH.

Music by
VICTOR HERBERT.

Bon Bon Buddy.

Words by
ALEX ROGERS.

Music by
WILL MARION COOK.

"Choc'-late drop," and "Bud-dy" seemed to stick to me some how,_____ Then
there was one called "Dummy Smith" and one called Ba - by Blue,"_____ And

some one add ed "Bon Bon," So here's what they call me now._____
they all used to tell me, "Bud its pret - ty soft for you."_____

Chorus.

Bon - Bon Bud-dy the choc - o - late drop,_____

Dat's me,_____ Bon - Bon Bud-dy is

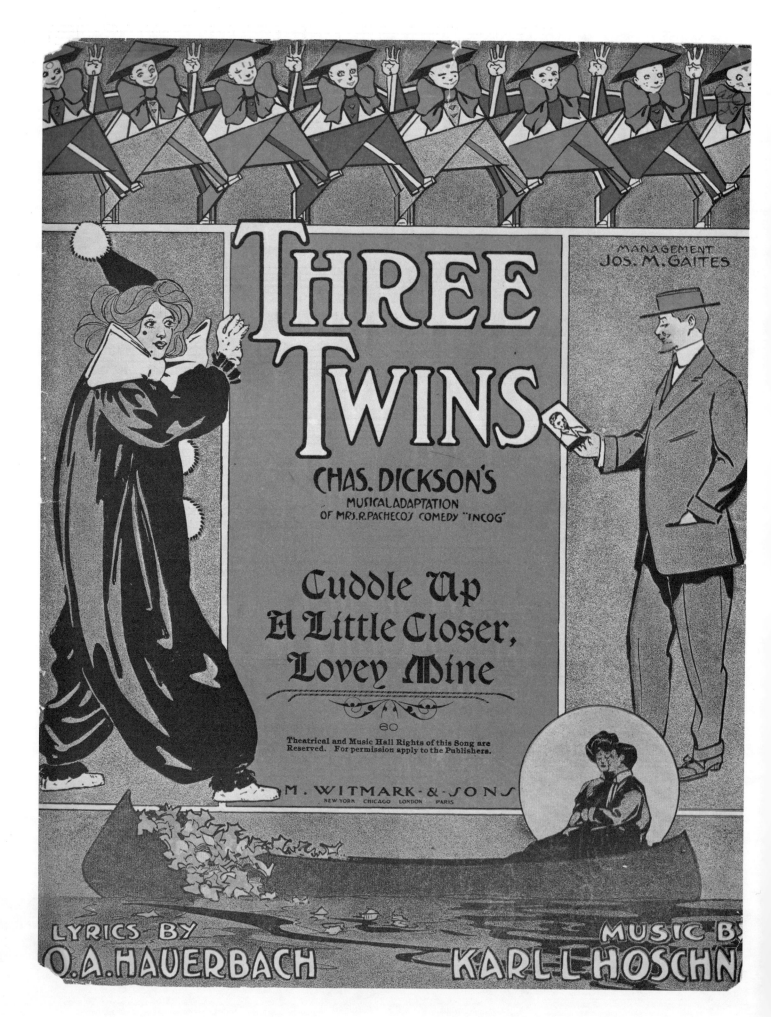

CUDDLE UP A LITTLE CLOSER, LOVEY MINE.

Lyric by
O. A. HAUERBACH.

Music by
KARL HOSCHNA.

Allegretto grazioso.

PIANO.

On the Sum-mer shore,— Where the break-ers roar,— Lov-ers
Then she deigned to rest,— On his man-ly chest,— Her dear

sat on the glist-ning sand._____ And they talked of love,— While the
head with its flow-ing curls._____ And she said, "I'd stay,— On this

moon a-bove,— And the stars seemed to un-der-stand._____ Then she
lap for aye,— How I en-vy the Cap-land girls._____ For Miss

grew more cold,_ And he grew more bold, Till she tho't that they had bet - ter
Es - qui - maux,_ 'Mid the ice and snow, Has no steam - heat when he comes to

go._____ But al - tho' he heard,_ He not e - ven stirred. On - ly
call._____ Not a sin - gle glim,_ So its up to him,_____ To

mur - mured in tones soft and low._____
whis - per in sum - mer or fall."_____

rall.

CHORUS. *Moderato.*

Cud - dle up a lit - tle clos - er, Lov - ey mine.

p *f a tempo.*

The "HIT" of Lew Fields' New Production
"The Girl Behind the Counter."

THE GLOW-WORM

"GLÜHWÜRMCHEN"
IDYL

BY

PAUL LINCKE

VOCAL

SONG. (High in F.) (English Words)		60
x SONG. (Medium in Eb.) "		60
SONG. (Low in C.) "		60
SONG. (High) (German Words)		60
SONG. (Medium) "		60
SONG. (Low) "		60
SONG. (Medium) (French Words)		60
TRIO. Female Voices & Piano (German Words)		1.00
MALE Quartette (English Words)		60
MIXED Quartette (German Words) Score		40
MIXED " " Separate Parts		50
FEMALE Quartette (German Words) Score		40
FEMALE " " Separate Parts		50
MALE " " Score		40
MALE " " Separate Parts		50
ZITHER (Treble Cleff) (German Words)		75

INSTRUMENTAL

PIANO SOLO—Original Arr.		60
PIANO SOLO—Simplified Arr.		60
FOUR HANDS.		1.00
VIOLIN SOLO.		50
SECOND VIOLIN.		50
CELLO.		50
FLUTE.		50
PIANO ACC. To Above.		60
SMALL ORCHESTRA.		75
FULL ORCHESTRA.		1.15
MILITARY BAND.		1.00
ORGAN. (15 to 31 Keys)		1.50

Also Published for	
MANDOLIN SOLO.	40
MANDOLIN & GUITAR.	50
MANDOLIN & PIANO.	65
TWO MANDOLINS & GUITAR,	75
TWO MANDOLINS & PIANO.	75
MANDOLIN, PIANO & GUITAR,	75
TWO MANDOLINS.	60
TWO MANDOLINS, PIANO AND GUITAR.	1.00
BANJO SOLO.	50
SECOND BANJO.	50
PIANO ACC.	50

Published by JOS. W. STERN & Co.

APOLLO VERLAG BERLIN

The Glow-Worm.

Song.

English Words by
LILLA CAYLEY ROBINSON.

Music by
PAUL LINCKE.

When the night falls si-lent-ly,___ the night falls si-lent-ly___ on for-ests
"Lit-tle glow-worm, tell me pray,___ oh glow-worm, tell me pray,___ how did you

dream-___ing, Lo-vers wan-der forth to see,___ they wan-der
kin-___dle, Lamps that by the break of day,___ that by the

forth to see___ the bright stars gleam-___ing; And lest they should
break of day,___ must fade and dwin-___dle?" "Ah, this se-cret,

lose their way,— lest they should lose their way,— the glow-worms night - ly
by your leave,—this se - cret, by your leave,— is worth the learn - ing!

Light their ti - ny lan-terns gay,—their ti - ny lan-terns gay— and twin-kle
When true lo - vers come at eve,—true lo-vers come at eve,—their hearts are

bright - ly. Here and there, and ev'- ry - where, from mos - sy dell and
burn - ing! Glow-ing cheeks and lips be - tray, how sweet the kis - ses

hol - low, Float-ing, glid - ing through the air, they call on us to
tast - ed! Till we steal the fire a - way, for fear lest it be

far we wan - der, Love's sweet voice is call - ing yon - der!

Ah

Shine, lit - tle glow - worm, glim - mer, 8----- shine, lit - tle glow - worm,

Ah

glim - mer! Light the path, be - low, a - bove, and lead us on to

8-----

rit.

mf

Love! Love!

D.S.

fz f fz

COHAN & HARRIS'S COMEDIANS present

GEO. M. COHAN'S
LATEST MUSICAL PLAY

FIFTY MILES FROM BOSTON

6

SONGS of the PLAY

JACK AND JILL
THE SMALL-TOWN GAL
HARRIGAN
AIN'T IT AWFUL
THE BROOKFIELD TWO-STEP
THE BOYS THAT FIGHT THE FLAMES
FIFTY MILES FROM BOSTON — SELECTION $1.00

F. A. MILLS
132 WEST 29TH ST.
NEW YORK

"Harrigan."

GEO. M. COHAN.

Moderato.

Who is the man who will spend or will ev - en lend?
Who is the man nev - er stood for a gad a - bout?

Har - ri - gan, That's me! ___ Who is your friend when you
Har - ri - gan, That's me! ___ Who is the man that the

find that you need a friend? Har - ri - gan, That's me! ___ For
town's sim - ply mad a - bout? Har - ri - gan, That's me! ___ The

I'm just as proud of my name you see, As an Em - per - or, Czar or a
la - dies and ba - bies are fond of me, I'm fond of them, too, in re -

King, could be: Who is the man helps a
turn, you see: Who is the gent that's de -

CHORUS.   SOLO.

man ev - 'ry time he can? Har - ri - gan, That's me!
ser - ving a mon - u - ment? Har - ri - gan, That's me!

CHORUS.

H - A - dou - ble R - I - G - A - N spells Har - ri - gan,

Proud of all the I-rish blood that's in me; Div-il a man can say a word a-gin me. H - A - dou - ble R - I - G - A - N, you see,_____ Is a name that a shame nev-er has been con-nect-ed with. Har-ri-gan, That's me!___ me.___

 *Harrigan* 23

Nº 1 in G  Nº 2 in A♭ 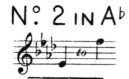 Nº 3 in B♭ 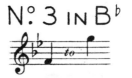 Nº 4 in C

SUNG BY

MR JOHN MCCORMACK
AND
MR DAN BEDDOE

I HEAR YOU CALLING ME

SONG

THE WORDS BY

HAROLD HARFORD

The Music by

CHARLES MARSHALL

PRICE 60 CENTS (NET)

BOOSEY & CO.

NEW YORK - TORONTO - LONDON (ENG.)
9 EAST 17TH ST.   RYRIE BLDG., YONGE ST.   295 REGENT ST., W.

ORCHESTRAL ACCOMPANIMENT TO THIS SONG IS NOW PUBLISHED IN ALL KEYS............ PRICE 60¢

I Hear You Calling Me.

~~~~~~~~~~~~~~~

I hear you calling me.
You called me when the moon had veiled her light,
Before I went from you into the night;
I came, — do you remember? — back to you
For one last kiss beneath the kind stars' light.

I hear you calling me.
And oh, the ringing gladness of your voice!
The words that made my longing heart rejoice
You spoke, — do you remember? — and my heart
Still hears the distant music of your voice.

I hear you calling me.
Though years have stretched their weary length between,
And on your grave the mossy grass is green:
I stand, — do you behold me? — listening here,
Hearing your voice through all the years between.

HAROLD HARFORD.

I Hear You Calling Me.

Words by
HAROLD HARFORD

Music by
CHARLES MARSHALL

mossy grass is green: I stand,........ do you be-hold me? list-'ning

here, Hear - ing your voice through all the

years be - tween........., I hear you

call - - ing me.....................

I LOVE YOU SO!
Valse Song

Words by
ADRIAN ROSS.

Arr. for Piano by H. M. HIGGS
On Melodies by Franz Lehár.

Gold — — en glow — — ing Lamps are

throw ing Light a - - bove, _____ While the

sway - - ing Tune is say - - ing Love, love, love! _____

_____ And the feet of danc - - ers Sound it

as they go _____ Don't you hear them say My

I'm Afraid to Come Home in the Dark

Respectfully dedicated to
Mr. Chas. Grapewin.

Words by
HARRY WILLIAMS.

Music by
EGBERT VAN ALSTYNE.

1. "Jones-ie" mar-ried Ma-bel, a wise old owl was he,___ He told his wife he nev-er drank a strong-er thing than tea,___ But
2. That night af-ter din-ner, he bade his wife a - dieu,___ Said she "Oh no, its dark and so I'm goin' to go with you",___ But
3. She kissed him good morning, to - see him she was glad,___ And when she tucked him up in bed says Jones "I guess I'm bad"___ Next

aft-er hon-ey mooning at night he stayed a-way, And for a week he
some-how Jonesy shook her for he was smooth as silk, He got home just in
day the same old sto-ry he came home just at dawn, But he got **so-ber**

nev-er got home 'till the break of day,— At last poor Ma-bel asked the rea-son
time to meet the man that brought the milk His wife stood wait-ing for him on the
right a-way when he found she was gone— At noon he heard her slam the gar-den

why_____ Said Jones "I'm goin' to tell the truth or die."_____
stair_____ While Jones-ie and the milk man sang this air._____
gate_____ Said she to Jones-ie "Is my hat on straight?"_____

CHORUS.

Ba - by dear, (sh) lis-ten here I'm a-fraid to come home in the
Ba - by dear, (sh) lis-ten here I'm a-fraid to come home in the
Ba - by dear, (sh) lis-ten here I'm a-fraid to come home in the

dark_____ Ev - 'ry day the papers say a Rob-ber - y
dark_____ Ev - 'ry day the papers say a Rob-ber - y
dark_____ Ev - 'ry day the papers say a Rob-ber - y

in the Park_____ So I sat a - lone in the Y. M. C. A.
in the Park_____ So I sat a - lone in the Y. M. C. A.
in the Park_____ So I sat a - lone in the C. A. F. E.

Sing-ing just like a lark_____ There's no place like
Sing-ing just like a lark_____ There's no place like
Sing-ing just like a lark_____ There's no place like

home_____ But I could-n't come home in the dark._____
home_____ But I could-n't come home in the dark._____
home_____ But I could-n't come home in the dark._____

I'm Afraid To Come Home In The Dark

Male Quartette

Arr. by RIBE DANMARK

JEROME. H. REMICK & CO. New York & Detroit.

ALL EYES ARE ON ANNA HELD
WHEN SHE SINGS

IT'S DELIGHTFUL TO BE MARRIED

Anna Held

IN "THE PARISIAN MODEL"

MANAGEMENT
F. ZIEGFELD JR.

WORDS BY
ANNA HELD

MUSIC BY
SCOTTO
AND
CHRISTINE

Published by JOS. W. STERN & CO. 102 104 W. 38TH ST. N.Y.
NEW YORK CHICAGO LONDON

LONDON JOS. W. STERN & CO.
ALBERT ? ON SIDNEY AUSTRALIAN N ZEND

60/5

"It's Delightful to be Married!"

Anna Held's Version of the Parisian Success,

"Petite Tonkinoise."

Words by
ANNA HELD.

Music by
V. SCOTTO.

In our schooldays,— mer-ry school-days,— We were hap-py girls and
Soon we mar-ried,— you and I, dear,— You to me and I to
When old age comes, to us both, dear,— We will still be in the

boys;—— We would al-ways play to-geth-er,—— And our
you,—— And we had a lit-tle home, dear,—— With just
game;—— I will be a gay old par-ty,—— You will

life was full of joys; And at play - time,___ in the
room e - nough for two; And a lit - tle,___ lat - er
be a grand old dame; And then arm in___ arm, to -

May - time,___ You and I were not a - part;___ I was
on, dear,___ Still more hap - py we would be,___ For we
geth - er,___ We will go to church right near,___ You will

then your school-boy lov - er, — You, my lit - tle girl sweet - heart.___
found our ti - ny cot - tage, Was a - bout the size for three.___
call me your old dar - ling, I will call you my old dear.___

It's Delightful to Be Married   43

44   *It's Delightful to Be Married*

It's Delightful to Be Married 45

Love is like a Cigarette.

De Lome and Male Chorus.

Lyric by
GLEN MAC DONOUGH.

Music by
VICTOR HERBERT.

in - cense mounts__ In swirl - ing curves a - bove,_____ And as I
- witch - ing shades!__ Each sad - ly smiles at me,_____ With each I

dream, My fan - cy turns to Love!_____
swore, To love e - ter - nal - ly!_____

(He rolls a cigarette)

Love is like a ci - gar - ette (A ci - gar - ette may last as long.)

pp molto delicato

A WALTZ DREAM

A VIENNESE OPERETTE

BOOK BY
**FELIX DORMANN &
LEOPOLD JACOBSON**

MUSIC BY
OSCAR STRAUS

ENGLISH BOOK & LYRICS ADAPTED BY JOSEPH HERBERT

VOCAL				
Waltz Duet-Love's Roundelay.	·	·	·	60
Kiss Duet-Sweetest Maid of All,	·	·	·	60
A Husband's Love,	·	·	·	60
Piccolo	·	·	·	60
Love Cannot be Bought,	·	·	·	60
Life is Love and Laughter,	·	·	·	60
A Country Lass and a Courtly Dame	·	·	·	60
Kissing Time,	·	·	·	60
The Family's Ancient Tree,	·	·	·	60
Two is Plenty,	·	·	·	60
INSTRUMENTAL				
Waltz Dream Waltzes,	·	·	·	60
March	·	·	·	60
Gavotte	·	·	·	60
Selection,	·	·	·	1.00
Complete Vocal Score,	·	·	·	2.00

Published by JOS. W. STERN & CO. 102 104 W 38 ST N.Y.
NEW YORK MAIN STERN BUILDING CHICAGO LONDON
LONDON, JOS. W. STERN & CO.
ALBERT & SON, SIDNEY, AUSTRALIAN AGENTS.

No. 7. Waltz Duet.

"Love's Roundelay."

(Niki, Montschi.)

Lyric by
JOSEPH HERBERT.

Music by OSCAR STRAUS
Arr. by A. CARROLL ELY.

The soft sum-mer twi-light was fad - ing, I sat in the gar-den a - lone;___ The zeph-yrs of night ser-e-nad - - ing The trees with their mys-ti-cal tone.___ The

Dedicated to Mr. Frank Croxton.

On the Road to Mandalay.

From Kipling's "Barrack Room Ballads."

OLEY SPEAKS

By the old Moul-mein Pa - go-da look-in' east - ward to the sea, There's a Bur - ma girl a -

Budd, Pluck-y lot she cared for i - dols when I kissed her where she stood On the road to Man-da - lay,— where the fly - in' fish - es play, An' the dawn comes up like thun - der out of Chi - na 'crost the bay.

VESTA VICTORIA'S
NEW SONGS

VESTA VICT...

Featured by the
FAMOUS ENGLISH COMEDIENNE ON HER THIRD AMERICAN TOUR

POOR JOHN!

BY

LEIGH & PETHER

Writers Of

"Waiting at the Church"

5

NEW YORK:
FRANCIS, DAY AND HUNTER
15, WEST 30th STREET.
(NEAR BROADWAY)
LONDON

"POOR JOHN!"

Written by
FRED W. LEIGH.

Composed by
HENRY E. PETHER.

I ought to think myself a luck - y girl, I know, 'Cos
As soon as she could get me all a - lone — oh, dear! She
She said, "Young gals to - day are all for out - side show; The

I'm en - gaged, but still, some - how, I don't think so.
asked so ma - ny ques - tions that I felt quite queer.
clothes you *see* may look all right — the *rest* — oh, no!"

Copyright MCMVI by Francis, Day & Hunter.

International Copyright Secured.

Francis, Day & Hunter, { LONDON, 142 Charing Cross Road, W.C.
{ NEW YORK, 15 West 30th. Street.

John — that's the name of my "fin - *nonce,*" you see —
Thought John too young to take a wife just yet;
What she was driv - ing at I soon made out;

There's no mis - take, he's ve - ry fond of me. He
Asked when and where it was that we first met. She
My style of dress was too re - fined, no doubt. Then

took me out for walks, and oh! he was so nice! He
said no girl could help but wor - ship her dear son,
all at once she gave a sigh, and cried, "Oh, lor! I

al - ways used to kiss me on the same place twice.
told me pret - ty plain - ly what a prize I'd won.
won - der what on earth he wants to mar - ry for!"

Oft - en in the park we would sit and spoon, And
Start - ed ve - ry slow, then she made a spurt, And
That was quite e - nough— up my tem - per flew; Says

rit.

I was oh! so hap - py till the oth - er af - ter - noon.
hoped that I knew how to put a tail - piece on a shirt.
I, "Per - haps it's so that he can get a - way from you!"

CHORUS. *2nd time f*

John took me round to see his moth - - er! His moth - - er! His

moth - - er! And while he in - tro-duced us to each oth - er, She

weigh'd up ev'-rything that I had on. She put me thro' a cross-exam-i-

na - - tion; I fair-ly boil'd with aggra - va - tion. Then she shook her head,

Looked at me and said, "Poor John! Poor John!" John!"

"POOR JOHN"

MALE VERSION

Words by
F. LEIGH

Music by
H. E. PETHER

✄ ✄ ✄ ✄ ✄ ✄

1

I've got a silly sister, and her front name's Jane;
We tried to get her married, but it's all in vain.
Just when we fancied ev'ry hope was gone,
She got her clutches on a chap called John,
She told us lots about him—said he was so nice
Because he used to kiss her on the same place twice.
Then there came a change—love was growing cold;
We asked her what had happened, and this sad, sad tale she told

CHORUS.

John took me round to see his mother!   etc.

2

Said Jane, "I won't be taken there again, no fear!
His mother asked me questions till I felt quite queer.
Thought John too young to take a wife just yet;
Asked when and where it was that we first met:
She said no girl could help but worship her dear son,
And told me pretty plainly what a prize I'd won.
Started very slow then she made a spurt,
And hoped that I knew how to put a tail piece on a shirt".

CHORUS

John took me round to see his mother!   etc.

3

His mother said young girls were all for outside show;
The clothes you see may look all right, the rest—oh, no'.
"I saw exactly what she meant;" cried Jane;
"My style of dress was too refined, that's plain"!
Then all at once she gave a sigh, and cried, "Oh, lor!
I wonder what on earth he wants to marry for!"
That was quite enough—up my temper flew;
Says I, "Perhaps it's so that he can get away from you!"

CHORUS.

John took me round to see his mother!   etc.

"Red Wing."

(An Indian Fable.)

Words by
THURLAND CHATTAWAY.

Music by
KERRY MILLS.

Moderato.

Slower than March time

There once lived an In-dian
She watched for him day and

maid, A shy lit-tle prai-rie maid, Who
night, She kept all the camp-fires bright, And

sang a lay, a love song gay, As on the plain she'd
un-der the sky, each night she would lie, And dream a-bout his

while a-way the day; She loved a ___ war-rior bold, this the
com-ing by and by; But when all the braves re-turned, the

shy lit-tle maid of old, But brave and ___ gay, he
heart of ___ Red Wing yearned, For far, far a-way, her

rode one ___ day to bat-tle far ___ a-way.
war-ri-or gay, fell brave-ly in ___ the fray.

CHORUS.

Now, the moon shines to-night on pret-ty

-far 'neath his star her brave is sleep - ing,_____ While Red Wing's.

-far 'neath his star her brave is sleep - ing,_____ While Red Wing's

weep - ing_____ her heart a - way._____

weep - ing_____ her heart a - way._____

School Days.

When We Were A Couple Of Kids.

By COBB & EDWARDS.

Sail to the old vil - lage school house, An - chor out
'Mem - ber the mead - ows so green dear, So fra - grant with

side the school door, _____ Look in and see, there's
clov - er and maize, _____ In - to new ci - ty lots and pre-

you and there's me, A coup - le of kids once more. _____
ferred bus'ness plots, They've cut them up since those days. _____

Chorus.

School - days, school days, dear old gold - en rule - days

a tempo.

p-f

Read - in' and 'rit - in' and 'rith - me - tic, Taught to the tune of a hick - ry stick, You were my queen in cal - i - co, I was your bash - ful bare - foot beau, And you wrote on my slate, I love you Joe, When we were a coup - le of kids. _____ kids. _____

D.C.

Shine On, Harvest Moon

Words by
JACK NORWORTH

Music by
NORA BAYES - NORWORTH

The night was might - y dark so you could
I can't see why a boy should sigh, when

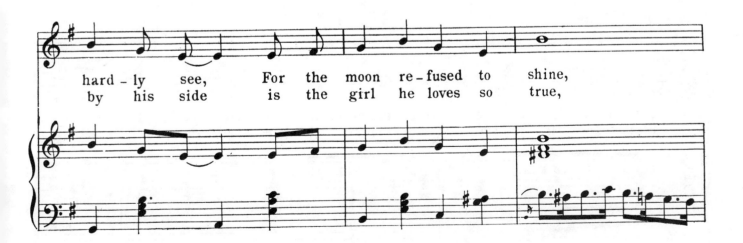

hard - ly see, For the moon re-fused to shine,
by his side is the girl he loves so true,

Cou – ple sit – ting un – der-neath a wil – low tree, For love they
All he has to say is "Won't you be my bride, For I love

pine,_____ Lit – tle maid was kind a – fraid of dark – ness So she
you,_____ Why should I be tell – ing you this se – cret When I

said, _____ "I guess I'll go," Boy be – gan to sigh,
know _____ that you can guess," Har – vest moon will smile,

Looked up at the sky, Told the moon his lit – tle tale of woe.____
Shine on all the while, If the lit – tle girl should an – swer "Yes."____

A SONG BY THE WRITERS ─of─ "SCHOOL DAYS"

SUNBONNET SUE

LYRIC BY
WILL·D·COBB

MELODY BY
GUS.EDWARDS

5

PUBLISHED BY
THE HOUSE MELODIOUS
GUS EDWARDS MUSIC PUB CO
1512 BROADWAY N.Y.

Sunbonnet Sue.

(When I was a Kid so High.)

Writers of "Schooldays."

Lyric by
WILL D. COBB.

Melody by
GUS EDWARDS.

So that is your new Sun - day
So that is your new Sun - day

bon - net?_____ Well, Sue, it's be - com - ing to you._____
bon - net?_____ Well, Sue, I must "hand it to you."_____

_ With those won - der - ful things you have on it,_____ You'll
_ It's a dream, and the day that you don it_____ They'll

89

make them "some jeal-ous," dear Sue;___ But some-how it
take them "some no-tice," dear Sue;___ But though it's a

sets me to dream-ing,___ Of the day we first said "How-dy-
crown for a queen dear,___ In my heart there's a soft spot or

do,"___ And I see you once more, In the bon-net you
two,___ For the knot that I tied, That tied my heart in-

wore, When I nick-named you "Sun-bon-net Sue."___
side, When I tied your old Sun-bon-net Sue.___

CHORUS. *Slowly - tenderly.*

Sun-bon-net Sue, Sun-bon-net Sue, Sunshine and ros-es ran sec-ond to you;

You looked so nice, I kissed you twice, Un-der your sun-bon-net blue.___ It was

on-ly a kind of a "kid kiss,"___ But it tas-ted lots nic-er than pie;___ And the

next thing I knew, I was dead stuck on you, When I was a kid so high.___ high.___

THE SENSATIONAL BASE BALL SONG

TAKE ME OUT TO THE BALL GAME

HENRY FINK

WORDS BY
JACK NORWORTH
MUSIC BY
ALBERT Von TILZER

5

THE YORK MUSIC Co
ALBERT VON TILZER, Mgr.
40 WEST 28TH ST. N.Y.

Dedicated to J. A. STERNAD.

Take Me Out To The Ball Game.

Words by
JACK NORWORTH.

Music by
ALBERT VON TILZER.

Copyright MCMVIII by The York Music Co.
Albert Von Tilzer Mgr.
40 West 28th St. New York.

blew_____ On a Sat-ur-day, her young beau
strong_____ When the score was just two to two,

called to see if she'd like to go, To see a show but Miss
Ka - tie Ca-sey knew what to do, Just to cheer up the

Kate said "no, I'll tell you what you can do:"_____
boys she knew, She made the gang sing this song:_____

CHORUS.

Take me out to the ball game, Take me out with the crowd_____

Oh, Fatherland

or

"To Maxim's Then I Go."

(Da geh' ich zu Maxim's.)

Translations by
GEORGE BONIFACE.

German Lyrics by
VICTOR LEON & LEO STEIN.
Music by FRANZ LEHÁR.

Fa-ther-land you cause by day a lot of trou - ble and dis-may, But
Va - ter- land, du machst bei Tag mir schon ge - nü - gend Müh' und Plag'! Die

night leads me, a dip - lo - mat, to serve my-self, I'm good at that! For
Nacht braucht je- der Di - plo - mat doch mei-sten-teils für sich pri - vat! Um

there's the Club's su-perb re-sort,   To which I al-ways go for sport; Tho' lit-tle
Eins bin ich schon im Bu-reau,   *doch bin ich gleich drauf an-ders - wo,*   *weil man den*

rest I find by day,   I make the night for it re-pay!   And
gan - zen lie-ben Tag   *nicht im-mer im Bu-reau sein mag!*   *Er -*

here and there I scat-ter cash;   A-mong the girls I cut a splash! And then I
stat - te ich beim Chef Be-richt,   *so thu' ich's mei-stens sel-ber nicht,*   *die Sprechstund*

oft - en treat - ies sign On ru-by lips, at this I shine! To
halt' ich nie - mals ein,   *ein Di-plo - mat muss schweigsam sein!*   *Die*

keep af-fairs of Na-tions right   I find it   takes time to in - dite,   and thus, like
Ac - ten häu-fen sich bei   mir,   ich fin-de,   s'gibt zu viel Pa - pier;   ich tauch' die

Dip - lo-mats I   know,   I vote the   mat - ter dull and slow.   'Tis
Fe - der sel - ten   ein   und komm doch   in   die Tint' hin - ein!   Kein

lit - tle won-der, so much thought   it takes, and   I was made for   sport;   And
Wunder, wenn man so   viel   thut,   dass man am   A - bend ger - ne   ruht,   und

that is why af - fairs of   state   I nev - er care to con-tem-plate.   To
sich bei Nacht, was man so   nennt,   Er - ho-lung nach der Ar - beit gönnt! Da

Ma-xim's then I go, Where I'm well known, you know. I'm wel-comed by the
geh' ich zu Ma - xim, dort bin ich sehr in - tim, ich du - ze al - le

a tempo

la - dies, So neat-ly each ar - rayed is, Lo - lo, Do-do, Jou-jou, Clo-
Da - men, ruf' sie beim Ko - se - na - men, Lo - lo, Do-do, Jou-jou, Clo -

clo, Mar - got, Frou - frou, And that's how I'm for - get - ting the
clo, Mar-got, Frou - frou, sie las - sen mich ver - ges - sen das

Animato.

dear old Fa - ther - land! Then cham-pagne gai - ly flows, And
teu' - re Va - ter - land! Dann wird cham-pa - gni - siert, auch

VILIA
Song

Words by
ADRIAN ROSS

Music by
FRANZ LEHÁR
Arranged for the Piano by
H. M. HIGGS.

once was a Vil - ia, A witch of the wood, A hunt - er be -

held her a - lone as she stood. The spell of her beau - ty up -

-on him was laid; He look'd and he long'd for the mag - ic - al maid!

For a sud-den trem - or ran, Right thro' the love-be-wil - der'd man,

And he sigh'd as a hapless lov-er can. "Vil - ia, O Vil - ia! 'he

witch of the wood! Would I not die for you, dear, if I could?

Allegretto

The wood-maid-en smiled, and no an-swer she gave, But beck-on'd him in-to the shade of the cave; He nev-er had known such a rap-tur-ous bliss, No maid-en of mor-tals so sweet-ly can kiss!

Soft - ly and sad - ly he sigh'd _____ "Vil - ia, O Vil - ia! the

witch of the wood, Would I not die for you, dear, if I could?"

"Vil - ia, O Vil - ia, my love and my bride!" Soft - ly and sad - ly he

sigh'd, Sadly he sigh'd, Vil - ia. _____

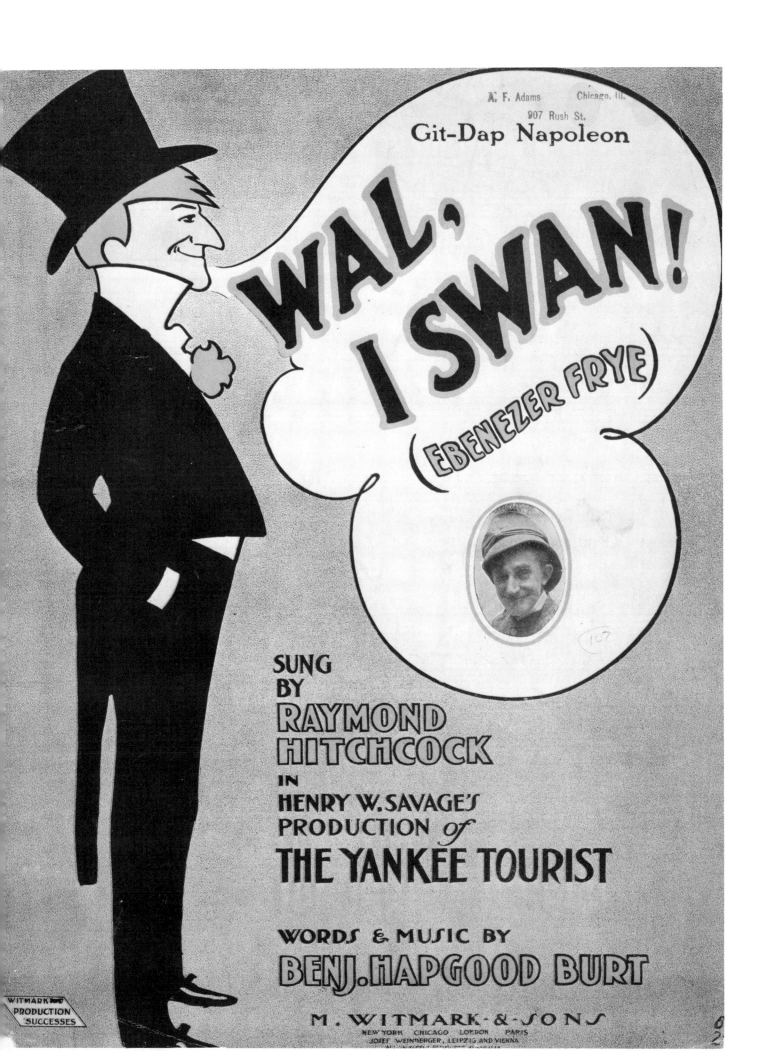

Wal, I Swan!

Ebenezer Frye.

Words and Music
By BENJAMIN HAPGOOD BURT.

I run the old mill o - ver here to Reub - en's - ville,
I drove the old mare o - ver to the Coun - ty Fair,
We had a big show here 'bout a week a - go,
I drove the old bay in - to town yes - ter - day,
My son Josh - ua went to Phil - a - del - phi - a

My name's Josh - u - a Eb - en - e - zer Frye.
Took first prize on a load o' sum - mer squash.
Pitched up a tent by the old mill dam.
Hitched by the track to the rail - road fence.
He would - n't do a day's work if he could.

I know a thing or two, you bet your neck I do, They
Stopped at the cid - er mill com - ing ov - er by the hill,
Ma says___ let's___ go in to the side - show, Jus'
Tied her___ good and strong, but a train___ came a - long, And
Smoked cig - ar - ettes___ too, way the cit - y folks___ do. What

don't ketch me for I'm too darn sly. I've seen Bun - co men,
Come home "tight - er" than a drum, by gosh! I was so durn full I
take a look at the tat - tooed man. I see a cus' look,
I ain't seen the "hoss" or the wag - in sence. Had to foot it home
he's a com - ing to,___ ain't no good. He didn't give a darn

al - lus got the best o' them, Once I met a coup - le on the
give a - way the old___ bull, Dropped both my reins___ clean out
sharp at my pock - et book, Says "gim - me two tens___
so I start - ed off a - lone, When a man says "Hur - ry! yer
'bout stay - in' on the farm, Keeps writ - in' hum___ he's a

Bos - ton train, They says "How be you!" I says "That-'ll do!
on the fill. Got hum so darn late could-n't find the barn__ gate.
for a five. I says "You durn fool! I be the con - sta - bule!
barn's on fire." But I had the key in my pock-et you__ see, So
doin' right well. It seems sort of fun-ny that he's al - lus out o' mon-ey,

Trav - el right a - long with your darn skin game."
Ma says, "Josh - u - a 'taint__ pos - *si - bil*."
Now you're a 'rest - ed sure__ as yer live."
· I knew that the cus' was a fool or a ·liar.
And Ma says the boy's up to some kind o' hell.

REFRAIN. *Rather slow.*

Wal, I swan! I mus' be git-tin' on! Git-dap, Na-po-le-on! it looks like rain. Wal,

mf

I'll be switched! the hay__ ain't pitched, Come in when you're over to the farm a-gain. *D.S.*
(3rd Verse.) durned! the but - ter ain't churned,

The Yama-Yama Man.

Lyric by
COLLIN DAVIS.

Music by
KARL HOSCHNA.

REFRAIN.

The Yama-Yama Mam.

EXTRA VERSES.

Lyric by
COLLIN DAVIS.

Music by
KARL L. HOSCHNA.

In the theatre now to-day,

Ev'ry girl takes off her hat.

But that doesn't help a bit,

For you can't see 'round her rat.

REFRAIN.

Mister Harriman to-day,

Thinks he'll have to change his dish.

Fridays he says he'll stick to meat,

For he's getting sick of "Fish."

REFRAIN.

Lady coming up the street,

Holds her skirt up with hands so deft.

To do this she has a perfect right,

And she also has a darn good left.

REFRAIN.

The "Pay-as-you-enter" car,

Is the brightest scheme evolved.

They can't *Miss* a nickel now,

So the traction question's solved.

REFRAIN.

YIP-I-ADDY-I-AY

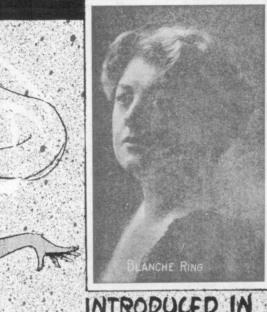

SONG SENSATION OF LONDON AND PARIS

BLANCHE RING

INTRODUCED IN AMERICA BY THE INCOMPARABLE BLANCHE RING IN JOE WEBER'S SATIRE "THE MERRY WIDOW AND THE DEVIL"

PUBLISHED BY
WILL D. COBB
Sole Selling Agent
"Shapiro" MUSIC PUBLISHER
Cor Broadway & Thirty Ninth Street
New York

LYRIC BY
WILL D. COBB
WRITER OF
WALTZ ME AROUND AGAIN WILLIE
SCHOOL DAYS ETC

MUSIC BY
JOHN H. FLYNN
WRITER OF
"ANNIE MOORE"

Yip-I-Addy-I-Ay!

Words by
WILL D. COBB.

Music by
JNO. H. FLYNN.

Tempo di Valse.

night he saw danc - ing, a maid so en - tranc - ing, His heart caught on
look not Spring Val - ley, to wel - come home Sal - ly, Who went to New
played and she tar - ried, that night they "got" mar - ried, But ev - en be -

fi - re in - side,_____ And mus - ic so mel - low he
York for the ride;_____ For the night that Von Bel - low cut
fore break of day,_____ Poor sleep - y Von Bel - low, heard

sawed on his cel - lo, She waltzed up to him and she cried:_____
loose on his cel - lo, She tore up her tick - et and cried:_____
his new wife yell - oh, "For good - ness sake, wake up and play!_____

CHORUS.

E__Yip - I - Ad - dy - I - Ay, - I - Ay! E__Yip - I - Ad - dy - I -

p - f